Living in Partnership with Spirit

Free range journaling for a deeper relationship with Source

Ingrid H. Turner
Bhava Spiritual Mission

Living in Partnership with Spirit is a work of my own creation.

The information in this book was correct at the time of publication, and the Author does not assume any liability for loss or damage caused by errors or omissions, again, this is my perspective, opinion, and experience, so it has been written as such.

ISBN - 978-1-961185-05-0

Cover, Book Design, and Layout by Ingrid H. Turner
ingridhturner.com | bhavamission.org

in omnia paratus publishing

www.inomniaparatuspublishing.com

www.ingramcontent.com/pod-product-compliance
Lightning Source LLC
Chambersburg PA
CBHW081006120626
46546CB00010B/3033
9781961185050